Grandparenting

With Grandma Fendell on the Way to School (and Other Studious Places)

Based on a True Story

By Charles Leahy, PhD

Illustrations by Sophia Chung

Copyright © 2023 Charles Leahy

All rights reserved.

To Lauren

Preface

The humorous stories found here are the result of a momentous change to the storyteller, a change known only to those grandparents who have lost a child. I felt the stories worth repeating because of the solo journey made by the teller, Grandma Fendell, and her redemptive practice to make the painful past into a joyful present.

New York City is a tough, flamboyant place even for a woman born in Brooklyn, who once lived in the City. She sold the house in Atlanta. She consigned or gave away the furnishings, cleaned-out the basement, and returned to the City where her daughter died.

She brought with her resolute courage, a first-rate mind, the resilience and knowledge of a doctor, and an exceptional ability to create imaginative childhood learning. Most of all, Grandma Fendell brought a well-spring of curiosity and humor, and an unconditional love for her grandchildren.

I hope you will find in these stories some atypical, creative and funny ways to engage in the world with children. As the scribe, I learned much more about where *learning* and *play* meet—much more than I ever knew as a parent.

Charles Leahy
Spring, 2023

An Introduction

"As dry leaves that before the wild hurricane fly," so the years passed since that long-remembered day at the Statue of Liberty. Miss Fendell, a high school teacher then, became a college Instructor, a doctor, a mother, and, finally, a grandmother.

Grandmother! That was an entirely new profession, she thought. Relatives, friends, elders, minors, book authors, famous grandparents all offered advice about: what to say, when to say it, gift-giving, spoiling, rules and regulations, foods and drinks, trips and vacations, school plays and school parades. The list was endless with proscriptions, warnings, advisory lists, health challenges and concerns, schoolmates, parent-grandparent relations. All a bit overwhelming if one paid too much attention—or not enough!

Grandma Fendell listened, reflected, read and, quite predictably, kept her own counsel. And because of that, she had many exceptional adventures, as you will see.

Chapter One
"One Fine, School Day"

In the beginning, for there must always be a beginning, *Miss* Fendell taught public school in a very large city. She taught or, perhaps, exposed is a better word her ninth-grade students basic science. She was a fine teacher based on all accounts from the school principal, other teachers, and, of course, the students who evaluated her through various expressions,

Happily, Miss Fendell acquired learning from the *emerging future* both inside and outside her classroom which was valuable then, and later. She combined this insight with her formal education in chemistry, biology and physics along with the "soft" skills (which always seemed particularly hard) of critical thinking, adaptability and problem solving.

She taught her science lessons cogently and well; and she had enough presence to adapt learning from the past and learning from the emerging future. For those not so familiar with semantics, the word "emerge", from the Latin *emergere,* means "bring forth, bring to light"; and, intransitively, "arise out or up, come forth, come up, come out, rise". All of which seemed to have happened one day to Miss Fendell in her ninth grade class, quite literally, through a proposal.

It was Tuesday, at exactly 2:59 in the afternoon, when the science class, with the section on biology, had nearly ended.

Miss Fendell turned to her class to complete the day's assignment and explained the requirement of drawing an amoeba cell. Out of the corner of her eye, she noticed a shy, but admiring student approaching. He hesitated, his words stuck, as he tried to ask a most serious question.

"Miss Fendell?" It was difficult to sense what Albert Vostick would say. "The Statue of Liberty," he blurted out, while Miss Fendell could not interpret what or how this was related to inspecting, then drawing, amoebas under a microscope.

Miss Fendell looked directly at Albert, imploring his question with her hand. "Yes?"

"Would you like to go to the Statue of Liberty with my parents and me?" Albert breathlessly asked. "They have been caretakers of the Statue for years and you could see it for free!"

Miss Fendell, surprised and smiling, paused as Albert squished his face. After a tense moment, and some logistical questions, she accepted the proposal for the following Saturday.

And so, on a sunny, breezy day in late afternoon, a curious teacher walked to Battery Park in the lowest part of Manhattan, and there at the waterfront, in what looked like a large rowboat with a motor, sat Albert and his father, waving.

Carefully climbing down the waterfront stairs, a slightly diffident, but venturesome, teacher stepped into the boat and greeted Albert and Mr. Vostick, who was at the controls.

Hrrrum! Hrrum!

The engine started, and the boat bounced over the choppy waters of New York Harbor with Miss Fendell, anxious and excited, looking up at Lady Liberty who loomed in the near distance ahead.

"...Miss Fendell, anxious and excited, looking at Lady Liberty who loomed in the near distance ahead."

On land, the Vosticks, including Mrs. Vostick, introduced themselves as Albert smiled proudly next to them. The group then smiled approvingly at one another. As Miss Fendell looked quickly around the area, she realized that, with the exception of Mr. and Mrs. Vostick and Albert, they were completely alone. Not another soul was on the island.

Mr. Vostick took charge. He moved directly toward the entrance of the Statue and entered the dimly-lit interior. After a few steps, while her eyes adjusted to the light, the cautious teacher paused involuntarily. There, in the middle of the Statue, was a staircase with hundreds of steps seemingly stuck in space, leading to an indistinct ceiling.

The scary, thrilled feeling at this site was interrupted by Mr. Vostick announcing, peremptorily, that he would lead the way.

Mr. Vostick, followed by Miss Fendell and Albert, began a jack-in-the-beanstalk climb to the Crown of the Statue. Up they went, their footsteps echoing on the metallic ladder, in the cool, cavernous interior of Lady Liberty's body. Three figures alone, breathing more heavily, up, up three hundred and fifty-four tin-ringing steps.

Nearly at the Crown, Mr. Vostick encouraged Miss Fendell, and they climbed higher, and higher.

The Crown was a study in light and perspective, twenty-five windows peering out on the dark harbor waters below, to New Jersey, or across to Staten Island, and the Atlantic Ocean and the world beyond!

After circling the Crown several times to view the world, Mr. Vostick faced Albert's teacher and, with a quizzical look, asked if she could go further. He pointed to an area set off from the Crown, an area forbidden to visitors with bold signs stating: "No Trespassing."

Not certain how or where they were to go, Miss Fendell blinked, then answered in the affirmative.

There, in the corner of the Crown, was a thin ladder leading up through the arm of Lady Liberty to the very top of the Statue. It led to the Torch held up over the Harbor, to the light that marked the Statue's beacon for boats, barges, tugs, and ocean liners coming to New York.

"You see, Miss Fendell, I have work to do up there, which should take just a few minutes, and I thought you might like to see the world from the highest point of the Statue."

To Miss Fendell, no modern Copernicus could have offered a more provoking perspective!

At the platform of the Torch, Mr. Vostick carefully maneuvered into position, and used a tool to replace one of the large lamps held in the Torch of Lady Liberty's hand. At the completion of the task, Miss Fendell, followed by Albert, obeyed the chief caretaker's order to begin a careful descent of the Statue. Down the narrow ladders and stairs, down hundreds of feet, their steps, again, echoed and reverberated in the deserted body of the Lady.

Back on firm ground, there was one more surprise in this exhilarating trip to the great Statue in the harbor. As the Vostick family gathered to say goodbye, Mr. Vostick, tall and alert, leaned over and said with a smile, "Miss Fendell, thank you so much for coming. Could I interest you in a small souvenir of your time with Lady Liberty?"

Before she could answer, Mr. Vostick pulled from behind his back, the actual two-foot electric bulb from the Statue's Torch and handed it to the surprised and delighted teacher!

As the boat made its way back to Battery Park and New York City, Miss Fendell cradled her souvenir securely in her arms. She realized she held a lamp seen by so many people, for so many years, who came to the country for so many different reasons. And they were guided by a lamp just like the one she held.

Miss Fendell rarely told people of her unique adventure and the gift she received. But she kept the precious light safely stored and always remembered its amazing origin.

On her way home that sunny fall day, she reflected on the visit: how learning requires a venturous mind and the risk of the untried—an assent to the emerging future. It also compelled listening and learning from others, including her students. It would help her later in her career, when listening to patients, and, yes, grandchildren, as they discovered the world!

Chapter Two

"A Morning of Stories, New and Old"

It was Tuesday, at 10:00 o'clock in the morning, and Grandmother Fendell had only minutes to get to the cozy classroom, filled with smiling book covers and (mostly) smiling children, for "Story Time."

Dashing down 72nd Street, they rushed over to 5th Avenue. Up they went, as the stroller containing Master Jake, the top of his winter cap fluttering with the sudden velocity, landed at the 81st Street entrance to the Metropolitan Museum of Art.

Grandmother Fendell blithely led her two-year-old grandchild into the Museum and within minutes, Master

Jake sat comfortably on the floor, next to a boy who seemed scared and wanted to hold his hand.

Grandma, thank goodness, was in the back of the class, smiling in approval of the warm setting, on-time arrival, and the friendly teacher's nods.

"Good morning Children," a benign voice said. "Thank you all for coming to Story Time. I think you will love our story this morning. It is about a very large animal whom most of the creatures in the forest loved. His name was Ralph, Ralph the Moose.

"He was very tall, taller than many of his friends who included: Freddy the frog, who admired Ralph's large appetite, the Wet People, the ducklings who loved rain, sprinklers, and ponds.

"They always watched how Ralph ate breakfast (from a tall ladder). Finally, there was Dewy, a water bird, who liked to fly to Ralph's shoulder and down to his plate, then open his beak and drink a drop of maple syrup. How delicious!

"Ralph the Moose, you see, only ate Pancakes which he or his friends made every morning. 1,000 pancakes, to be exact! In order to do so, Ralph had to climb a very large ladder so he could reach the top of the mountain of pancakes. As his friends gathered around him at the bottom of the ladder, Ralph deftly poured maple syrup over the wonderful towering plate of pancakes, forming a kind of gentle waterfall of syrup."

Oh, what delicious fun the children had at Story Time that Tuesday morning. But it was over shortly, and Grandma Fendell had to decide what to do and where to go next.

Serendipitously, just in front of her, was the answer. As Master Jake sat up straight in his stroller and stared at Grandma, she nodded her head and winked at him, then pushed his cart straight into a strange, and mysterious adventure.

Into the Greek and Roman Antiquities Gallery they strolled, a world of stone figures standing, leaning, sitting, and looking at them from pedestals above their heads! What could this place be that few children had ever seen before?

As they moved among the statuary, a Greek woman from the 4th century BCE greeted them; the folds of her marble

dress seemed almost real. A man standing near the entrance looked down on them, there were figures or heads everywhere, grey and white, when Grandma stopped and asked, "What are these figures, Jake? Who Are They? Where did they come from?" She stooped down to the staring grandchild.

"These are images of real people," she explained, "who lived thousands of years ago, so they are very, very old. They were made by a man who shapes people out of marble stone. He creates a statue so that the person will be remembered and might live forever."

Then, gently, looking at Jake and again at a statue, she asked, "Jake, what do you notice is missing from the figure of this man?"

Jake, looked, and then looked again, and said, "Grandma, he has no arms!"

"Yes, that is exactly correct."

"And what do you notice about the lady from ancient Greece?" she asked as they paused in front of her.

"Grandma, grandma, she has no head!"

"Oh dear," said Grandma, "that is very true."

And so, they went from statue to statue, and talked about the stone and the texture of the statue; about what happened to the arms and legs that had been lost over time; how strong the men looked, and how beautiful the women with heads looked.

On they roamed, grandmother and grandson, through magnificent galleries until they arrived at their last stop in front of an enormous, and very famous painting.

The painting was so large that it filled almost the entire wall of a room in the American Art Gallery. And so, Grandma and Jake had to stroll slowly alongside of the picture, so they could identify some of the objects. There was:

- A boat
- There was a man—two men—standing up
- There were men in the boat holding what seemed to be sticks
- There was water
- There were big chunks of ice

"Grandma, where's the Rainbow?" which Grandma had deftly pointed out.

As they walked from the gallery, George Washington was still standing up in the boat, still crossing the ice-chunked river heading to Trenton, his flag flying, a rainbow above promising hope, Grandma said, for the journey.

What a morning it had been. As Master Jake lay down for his nap, his eyes straining to stay open, he asked Grandma to tell him more about the statues and the people they saw, and about rainbows.

Chapter Three
"Grandma's Museum," as reported by Jake

Grandma lives only ten minutes from us. Lilla, my little sister, and I can walk out of the lobby door to 75th street, turn right, and go straight for three blocks to her apartment. We live only minutes apart, and in an apartment, too, but entering Grandma's building is like entering a museum.

We are greeted in the lobby by Grandma, but also by the elevator operator, Carlos. "Good afternoon, Lilla and Jake, would you like to help me drive the elevator today?"

"Yes, yes!" We jump up and down in delight.

With the help of Carlos, Lilla and I have to turn the large lever that shuts an iron gate in front of the elevator. We can see through the bars of the gate. It feels like we are in a prison—but only for a minute—especially as the gate clanks shut.

But I'm not scared, though I was a bit the first time we did it.

Lilla, Carlos, and I then turn the lever back the other way, and the elevator door closes on us with a swoosh and a loud clang! We then push the floor button marked "9", and we are off to Grandma's apartment.

When we reach her floor, clang goes the elevator door again, and we get out in a small hallway with a dark staircase.

Grandma told us that the staircase is an exit that leads all the way down to the bottom floor of the building.

We've used the elevator many times, but it always feels like a strange and exciting ride!

Looking out from inside Grandma's apartment, we can see skyscrapers of all different sizes and shapes—square, triangular, rounded, pyramid-like, and one with cake-like shapes at the top—all towering over us. And at night, we stare out the windows at all the colored lights: red, white, blue, and orange on Halloween! All these gigantic buildings stare at us in the dark. But they're friendly, and we wave at them—at the imaginary and real people who live or work there.

But more than the buildings, it's Grandma who creates the world we've entered. It sort of reminds me of the stage we have at school, where we act out different scenes and activities. Instead of a teacher, we have Grandma! She acts like a magician, turning the bathtub water for us into purple and pink waves; making a volcano that bubbles with red lava; turning her living room into a baseball field—a baseball field, if you can believe it!

The baseball field happened when Lilla and I complained that we missed playing baseball, and that kids can't play baseball inside an apartment on the 9th floor in an old New York City building. That's when Grandma stepped in with her special house rule: "No complaining!"

What happened next really surprised us. Grandma exclaimed, "Let's make a baseball field!"

"But, Grandma, we have no bats. We have no bases; we don't even have a ball. We can't make a baseball field!"

That's when Grandma put her arms around us and whispered, "Imagine!" That's what she said. "Imagine what we can use instead of a real bat or a real base?"

There was a minute or so of silence while we stared at her, then she got us started. "Jake, would you please get the broom from the closet?"

"Lilla, what could we use for bases?"

Lilla knew what real bases looked like and said, "Could we use paper plates, Grandma? Maybe small pillows?"

"That's great imagination! Lilla, will you bring some pillows from the bedroom?"

We both ran to find what we needed: four pillows—I mean "bases"—and one broom which became the bat. Grandma found a red, rubber ball somewhere.

I laughed as we set up our baseball field in Grandma's living room, way up in the air, over 72nd street, in a small apartment in an old building in New York City, and right in front of the green living room couch!

"Lilla, you're up first," I said and handed her the broom.

"Jake, you're the pitcher," instructed Grandma. "I'll play outfield."

Woosh! Lilla swung the broom and hit the ball over Grandma's head. She ran to first base amid screams of laughter. I was up next, excited by the diamond and the field we set up in Grandma's living room. I even imagined that some of the people in those other buildings were fans watching us!

As you can see, Grandma had very different rules than the ones other parents or grandparents had. I mean, she was strict about our behavior, our manners, and our treatment of each other. But we were allowed to have more fun there than almost anywhere else.

We loved getting our bedtime bath in a tub filled with pink and purple water—and bubbles! As we got into the tub, ready to be scrubbed, and educated, Grandma's voice became serious. "You have to clean yourselves tonight." And she handed each of us a can of Shaving Cream!

It was like having a squirt gun with cream in it. We could shoot it harmlessly at each other, make mustaches if we wanted to, or rub it all over. That's how we "cleaned ourselves," and Grandma laughed with us as we did it.

Of all the things we do at Grandma's apartment—and which we don't do anywhere else—one of the best is a pretty difficult and very, very fun scavenger hunt.

Woosh! Lilla swung the broom and hit the ball over Grandma's head. She ran to first base amid screams of laughter.

I don't mean just a list of places—"go here" "go there." Lilla and I are given *clues* and, sometimes, *riddles* about where to go which we have to figure out.

"Where is the drawer that holds the pan used for baking cookies?"

"What do you find when you look at the photo of your uncle and your two cousins?"

"Where is the space from which you can see a pizza restaurant below?"

And there are rhyming clues, too!

"Glad you're strong and able, you'll find the clue under the brown _____."

"There once was a country bumpkin, who found a clue by the _____."

We have to decide what room to go to, and the exact place to search. There we'll find the next clue, like behind my Uncle Josh's photo, so we can continue our hunt.

As we race from kitchen to bedroom, and back to kitchen, then on to bathroom, living room, hallway, and closet, somehow we can't stop laughing. We yell back and forth to each other, all the time knowing that when we succeed, there are surprising presents waiting for us!

Not just candy—we always love candy—but, on special occasions, I've gotten a Lego toy, and Lilla has gotten a little doll she can dress up. We never know what the prizes will be for finishing the scavenger hunt.

We love having to think, and figure out the clues, then run around, anxious to find all the secret places that Grandma has used for us to solve the puzzle. She makes us into little elementary detectives!

We never know exactly what Grandma has planned for us when we visit, but we always know it will be fun. We have the usual planned activities for kids: like sports we practice, music lessons, playdates, and birthday parties. But Grandma takes us to unusual places that surprise us; she teaches us school subjects *outside of school*; and she helps us learn and play in unusual ways, and at unusual times.

Chapter Four
"An After-Dinner Discussion of Some Physical Importance"

Shortly after dinner, and before any planned bedtime activities could take place, Jake and Lilla sat at the table and had nothing to do. They had a disinterested audience, and, as children are wont to do, especially when they feel silly, they began to laugh. And while laughing, they broke into a chorus—more like a chant of words, which they thought were very funny.

At the top of their lungs, they shouted:

"Poop! Poop! Poop! Poop!" This went on for quite a while.

The looks and expressions of disapproval on family members and guests were expected. An older cousin glanced at the ceiling in dismay; another diner raised his eyebrows as he stared at the children; a third pleaded for them to stop and said, "that's not nice to say."

Again, they chanted, "Poop! Poop! Poop! Poop!"

Jake and Lilla laughed even harder than before. As the children looked around, no one quite knew what to do.

Scold them and put them to bed early?

Ask them to apologize for shouting and saying nasty things?

Penalize them with no dessert if they did not immediately stop?

Amidst the noise, dismay, and even some laughs among the adults, something occurred which immediately ended the histrionics, the dismay, and the peals of laughter from the children.

A firm and direct voice said loud enough for everyone to hear, "Lilla and Jake: Where does poop come from?"

Everyone, everything—even the ticking clock—seemed to stop.

The children looked at Grandma, for it was she who posed this question, and Grandma looked at the children. The children, the adults, the clocks, all paused.

Who *could* answer this question, the children wanted to know. The adults wanted to know *who would?*

And so, Grandma began to ask Jake and Lilla the question directly, again.

"Where does poop come from?"

The children, who thought they knew, answered "Food!"

"Correct Answer," Grandma said.

"And what do you do with food? Where do you put it?"

"In your mouth," said Jake with certainty.

"Yes."

"And where does it go after you put it in your mouth?" Grandma pointed to her throat.

The challenge was on about the journey, and the travel destiny, of what? *Poop!*

"The throat" came back in unison from the children. And another correct answer provoked smiles all around.

"When the food enters your mouth, what do you do?"

"Chewing" was quickly agreed upon.

And then Grandma introduced a concomitant topic, which increased attention around the small dinner table that evening.

She explained that chemicals called enzymes are released as you chew the food into smaller pieces, so that your body can begin to absorb the nutrients into your blood, to make you strong and grow.

"From your throat", she continued, "your hamburger, now in smaller pieces, gets pushed—*don't forget to swallow*—to the esophagus, a wonderful muscular tube. And the esophagus pushes your hamburger to where?" Grandma pointed to her stomach for emphasis.

"Our tummies!" the two happily replied.

"So, you chew your food in the mouth, which passes to the throat, and through the esophagus, to the stomach. And at each place, something is happening—a chemical reaction, a muscular reaction—to your food as it gets separated into good particles and waste particles."

"This," Grandma paused, "is where it gets really interesting!"

No one who was present that day could have guessed they would be taken on a travel narrative of the body's digestive system! And, perhaps, no one would have guessed that it could hold everyone's attention – perhaps more than anyone, the children—for what seemed several minutes.

"Your stomach not only holds food, it grinds food, and adds acids and enzymes that break that hamburger into a liquid paste."

She paused again and looked fixedly at the children. "Where, Jake and Lilla, does it go after the stomach?"

No one exactly knew, except Grandma. And Grandma was right; it wasn't just interesting, it was amazing!

"It goes into your small Intestine. It is there that the nutrients in your food get processed into your blood stream."

"Now, do we have a measuring tape in the house?" Grandma looked at the adults, who in a matter of moments, brought a large metal tape from somewhere in a kitchen drawer.

"Lilla, would you please hold the tape measure? And Jake, please pull the end of the tape out to exactly 22 feet?"

As they spread out across the room, they could not imagine why Grandma had asked them to perform this feat (which is, by the way, a lovely pun!)

"22 feet, okay?" Grandma smiled, then pointed to the area below her stomach. "This is where your small intestine is located, and it could be 22 feet long, zigzagging downward."

"Grandma", exclaimed Jake, "that can't be possible. I'm too small!" Then Lilla said, "I'm too small!" The adults said, "that's too long!"

Grandma said to Jake and Lilla, "You are correct, but by the time you grow up, it could be 22 feet long."

She then continued, "So, where does poop come from? In the small intestines, food gets separated; the nutrients go into the bloodstream, but there it separates out the waste from the nutrients."

The audience could see Grandma warming to the finale. "The waste goes from the small intestine to the _____." Grandma waited for the missing words to be filled in, and a chorus of voices responded with, "Large Intestine!"

"Finally, the long journey ends, and the waste—the poop—goes to your rectum or anus and, plop—plop, poop!"

There was a momentary pause, and then spontaneously, everyone clapped and cheered. "Yay Grandma! Yay Grandma! Yay Poop!"

That night, as the children went to bed, and some of the adults walked home, they knew they had learned a lesson—several lessons about unexpected outcomes: about children's behavior, about human and, yes, emotional chemistry. More than all that, they learned how science education is taught by Grandma.

Chapter Five
"A Postscript to the Dinner," as reported by Jake

As you might have guessed, there was also another side to Grandma. We learned that she was a scientist and a doctor and, I think now, she was most of all, our teacher—though she never said that.

One day, not long after she explained our digestive system, we were at Grandma's apartment, when she asked us to stand up next to each other. She then left the room and came back in a few minutes with something odd around her neck.

She held up an instrument and asked, "What person whom you have visited has used one of these? And what is it called?"

We remembered the doctor used this funny-looking tool on our chests, but we couldn't remember the name of it, if we ever knew.

Grandma explained it was a stethoscope, and that it was used to listen to our heart. She said it was also used to listen to our lungs, our stomachs, and our intestines.

She then bent down and placed what she called the resonator (the small metal piece at the end of the tubing) on my heart, then on Lilla's. She declared that our hearts sounded very well.

Right after her heart-readings, Grandma took off the stethoscope and put it around Lilla's neck.

"Time for you, Dr. Lilla, to listen to your brother's heart to hear how it sounds." Grandma carefully placed the stethoscope's hearing buds in Lilla's ears, and then, placed the resonator on my heart!

"Lub, dub, lub, dub," Lilla exclaimed. "His heart is beating very loudly—maybe he's sick."

Grandma, then listened again, and proclaimed that my heart was beating normally, and at the right sound level. I was perfectly fine!

"Dr. Jake, it is now your turn to check your sister's lungs."

I put the earpieces in my ears, and Grandma placed the resonator at just the right place to listen to Lila's lungs.

"Lilla, will you please cough loudly?"

"Yikes," I said. "That was loud!"

"And, was it clear, or was there a gurgling or raspy sound?" Grandma made sounds like "gurgling water" and then hissing or scratchy sounds. "Dr. Jake please check your sister's back, on both sides, and ask Lilla to take a *deeeeep* breath and blow out."

Lilla and I both practiced, and listened, and pronounced our opinions.

It was at this point in our medical examinations that Grandma really proved to us that the grumbling and grinding sounds of our stomachs and intestines were caused by us—digesting food. I thought, oh my, we could hear where poop really comes from!

Grandma called it the "bowling alley," and when Lilla and I listened, we were surprised, at the noise. We joked and laughed about the sound of food, and poop, but also about what real doctors do.

I was pretty sure I understood about the digestive system, but I knew there was something very different between Grandma telling us about it and Grandma showing us about it.

I remember, too, as Grandma was putting away the stethoscope, she mentioned that if the doctor does not hear any of the sounds we heard, that it could indicate a problem, an obstruction or blockage in the stomach that could prevent going to the bathroom. And, so, listening with the stethoscope was a very important practice of doctors.

As we walked home that day with Grandma, Lilla and I talked about how we wanted to tell all our friends about what we did, how we did it, and how we imitated a real doctor visit.

Chapter Six
"*Grandparenting* on the Way to School"

Grandma Fendell had a marked propensity for walking the grandchildren to school daily, rain or shine, unless instructed otherwise.

A walk to Jake and Lilla's school—some would call it a hike—left on 75th Street, right to Park Avenue, left on 95th almost to Madison. A total of 3.3 miles, round trip.

A walk in New York City is an adventure in noise (firetrucks, busses, cars, people), space (shops, skyscrapers, bridges, sidewalks), physical effort (down to subway, up to bus steps, rain, and snow), and emotional inputs (blazing signs, shop windows, traffic patterns, crowds).

The environment of the city is always changing and always staying the same. So Grandma encouraged her grandchildren to become aware of the environment of a cityscape and the variations they were encountering each day.

Jake and Lilla discovered there was a lot to learn just by walking to school and looking at things they hadn't noticed or thought about before.

Shivering one morning amidst a gray cloudy sky, Jake noticed that the tops of some skyscrapers were "scraping" the clouds and could hardly be seen, while others were covered by thick white clouds, and the tops could not be seen at all.

Jake was already interested in environments and atmospheres. He had flown in a plane, been high up in a skyscraper, and been down below in a subway. In what atmosphere was that skyscraper hidden by clouds? What atmosphere were he—and Grandma in? Was the skyscraper in the stratosphere? How could they find out?

Grandma explained the science, that earth was surrounded by one atmosphere, but composed of many levels.

Grandma had a refrain which worked like magic for finding information that Jake and Lilla wanted to know. "Let's ask Professor Google." In that way, they both became proficient in using their smart phones—asking and receiving answers to really good questions!

When they reached Park Avenue, Grandma excitedly told them there were, "In fact, five major levels which composed the Earth's atmosphere, each with its own name, height, and environment."

"What level are we in?" asked Jake.

"What a great question. I'm happy to answer it. And please, keep your hat on; it's cold," Grandma cautioned.

"Believe it or not, we're in the exact same level as those skyscrapers. It's called the troposphere." She paused and then pronounced each syllable. "Tro – Po – Sphere."

"Tro-po-sphere" the children chanted back!

"When you see those puffy clouds in the sky, or rain or snow coming down, or birds flying above, you're living in the troposphere. It's the best sphere for humans to live in because here we can breathe air naturally and survive—without a spacesuit!

As they walked along talking, Jake suddenly had lots of questions. "Where's the stratosphere, Grandma? Where was I when I flew to California? And where did the spaceship go--the one you taught me to count backwards from ten before it took off?"

They all paused to glance at Grandma's smart phone, for just a few minutes, to look at the levels pictured that surrounded the earth and that the "Professor" had so kindly brought to the phone screen.

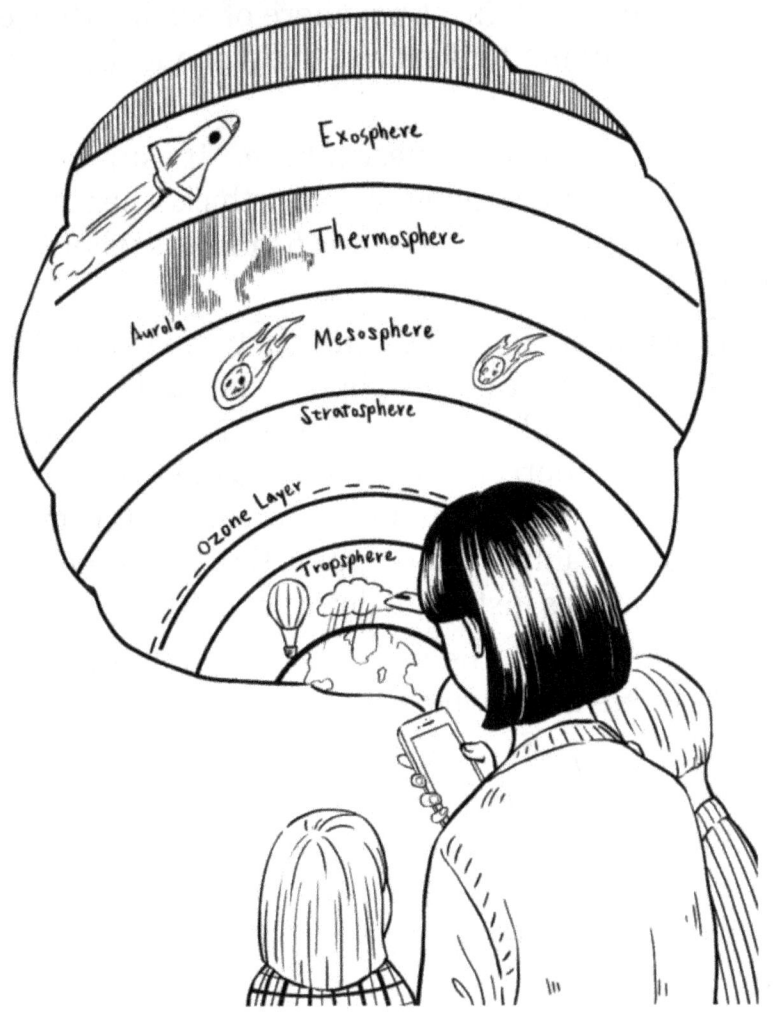

One question led to lots of other questions, as Grandma increased the pace of walking.

"Remember, the stratosphere is the layer surrounding earth above the troposphere where we are. That layer is 22 miles thick, and there are no storms or turbulence there to mix up the air.

The plane to California flew in the lower stratosphere—so you and Lilla and Daddy wouldn't bounce up and down all the way there!"

By the time Jake and Lilla reached their school, the children had heard about fascinating differences between the layers composing the atmosphere of earth. While eyeing her phone, Grandma told them briefly about the layers beyond.

"Next comes the mesosphere. It surrounds the stratosphere and is also about 22 miles thick. The air is so thin we couldn't breathe there. The mesosphere is where you can see meteors and shooting stars!"

The children liked hearing that; they loved to see shooting stars. "The thermosphere," she said, "comes next, and that layer is—oh my goodness—319 miles thick! Our layer, the troposphere, is only 5-9 miles thick. But there's an even bigger difference. The temperature in the thermosphere is 4,500 degrees Fahrenheit! Compare that to our temperature this morning; it was just 46° Fahrenheit."

Grandma faced them with her hand raised. "Most surprising to me is knowing that is the very place where the international Space Station circles the earth!" That came as a surprise to the children, too.

"Way, way up in the Earth's atmosphere, is the exosphere, and it is the final edge between our level (the troposphere) and outer space. It is 6,200 miles thick. It is a huge part of Earth's environment and the astronauts have to go through all these layers to get to outer space."

She looked at them and smiled. "There are other layers, but we're at school."

The grandchildren hugged Grandma goodbye before they went in the school door. They turned around just before going in, and Jake shouted back, "Grandma, what's beyond outer space?"

Perhaps Jake put it best when asked about walking to school: "We learned a lot; how to tell how old trees were, the names of flowers that we liked, and why there were so many ambulances in front of a hospital. Grandma made us think about things, and we made Grandma think about things. Usually, the questions were about places and objects that were right in front of us. Like the traffic jam we saw one day."

It was on 82nd street. A garbage truck was making a pickup on its usual route when traffic suddenly stopped. Within minutes, every type of car or truck or van was stuck, each driver honking, waving, looking around, cursing, pleading, praying, to get out of, around, or through the traffic jam.

"What would you do if you were stopped in a traffic jam behind a garbage truck?" asked a familiar voice from the clamorous troposphere they found themselves in on the way to school.

"I'd go around it," said Lilla.

"But you can't go around it. Everyone is blocked in."

"I'd honk my horn and make it so loud that the garbage truck would have to move," said Jake.

"But that's what everyone seems to be doing, and it isn't helping."

"I'd call the police. I'd...."

Grandma didn't speak for what seemed a long time, so they kept walking. She looked like she was thinking.

Finally, she said, "There's another way of dealing with your car that is stopped, waiting for a garbage truck to move."

The children noticed Grandma's voice changed when she had something important to say. Her tone lowered and she made gestures with her hands, pointing to herself.
"What can we–Jake, and you Lilla, and I—do to become patient and calm ourselves when we have to wait—longer than what we want to—for a friend to come over, a teacher to call on us, or a traffic jam behind a garbage truck to end?"

And then, Grandma really surprised them, so much so that they stopped walking, and turned to look up at her, when she said, "We can learn to breathe!"

"Grandma, Grandma, we are breathing; we know how to breathe!" Lilla protested.

"That's true, but I am talking of a different way to breathe, in which you slow your breath down, and breathe from your tummy, and count your breaths. You would be able to calm yourself down, right in the middle of anxious or boring times—but it takes practice. It's called meditation, and I will teach you after school one day just how to do that."

Ironically, everyone was almost out of breath by the time they got to school, having watched that silly garbage truck, all that traffic down 82nd street, and all those angry people. All that, and they'd had to hurry to get there on time.

Though good as her word, it was not till Saturday night, when the children stayed over at her apartment, that Grandma taught them how to "breathe". It was right before going to sleep, when life had quieted down (if it really ever quiets down in New York City), and Grandma sat cross-legged on the bed.

Jake and Lilla happily decided to sit on the bed and fold their legs, too! They then learned how to breathe.

"First, we need to take a deep breath." Grandma took a deep breath.

"Now, breathe in slowly and deeply. Pretend you're going to blow up a balloon so that it gets very big.

Now, breathe out very slowly, so the balloon does not pop."

Jake and Lilla did their best.

"Let's try together," Grandma said, "and watch your tummy move in and out…"

The children laughed and tried again to blow up imaginary balloons, following Grandma's lead.

"Each time you breathe in and then breathe out, count, starting at 1 and ending at 10."

And so they practiced taking breaths, watching their tummies move up and down, and laughing at this new way to breathe. They also learned to hold their fingers (a thumb and a ring finger) together, to still their hands. It was fun. Then they all went to bed. *

On a waning day, the autumn moon just appearing, the low-lit room with human shadows reflected on the wall, the children sat cross-legged on the bed with their hands clasped in front of them, breathing and counting slowly. It lasted just a few minutes. They all were, in those minutes, calm, just breathing, reaching ten.

*Based on "The Basics of Meditation for Kids of Any Age",
https://www.healthline.com/health/meditation-for-kids

Chapter Seven
"I Don't Like Kandinsky!" and other Perspectives

1789 BURNS *Let. to Mrs. Dunlop* 4 Mar., As a snail pushes out his horns, or as we draw out a perspective.
The Oxford English Dictionary

"Perspective" is historically a difficult topic for great thinkers, art critics and poets, let alone children. Height counts here, if you are 3'10" or 6'7"; empirical experience counts here; linear versus systems thinking counts here; cultural norms count here, visual instruments count here....

Jake and Lilla had many regularly scheduled events in their regularly scheduled lives. There was school, of course, and there were: baseball and soccer practice (and games), tennis lessons, swimming lessons, religious classes, dance lessons, music lessons, doctors' appointments, playdates, and more. Helped by a parent, teachers, coaches, relatives, friends, doctors, therapists, etc., all aimed at instructing, directing, coaching, correcting, curing, improving, convincing, complying, and, sometimes punishing.

Distill it all, and a central question arises: how does one teach perspective? Or, in this case, how does a Grandmother teach perspective in light of all those others offering perspectives of their own?

And. then, when a sporting question arises?

A gym is not generally an aromatic venue. Even small children sweat as they learn the basics of swinging, serving, chasing after lobs, and hitting ground strokes on the courts of the East Tennis Club. It was of particular benefit that Jake learn a lifetime sport, one which might teach him to stay fit, create friends in friendly competition, or, consolidate a deal as a CFO.

On a particular day, Jake went to his tennis lesson as usual, but on this day, he would learn about life from a different angle.

The lesson just over, and the players still stimulated by the activity, or just fooling around, Jake's best friend caught him by surprise.

In the noisy, hot air of the gym, Max somehow found a hose. Not ready to end the fun, Max turned on the hose, and gleefully sprayed Jake from head to toe! The laughter and squirting only lasted a few minutes, but it caused Jake to become upset, then irate, and then close to tears in anger.

"Stop! Stop!" Jake screamed, as Max danced around him with the hose, enjoying the fun of spraying and watching the contortions of his friend. Jake tried to escape, but the other boy and hose followed him relentlessly.

The coach eventually spotted the surprise attack, and separated Max from the hose, after turning it off.

But Jake stood distraught, in soaking wet gym clothes, and looking for an adult to run to for retribution, for something to remedy the injustice.

Almost in tears, Jake blurted, "I don't want him for a friend. How could he be so mean? It's not right'..." as Grandma helped him out of the wet gym clothes and into his dry street clothes. "I'm never going to talk to him again. He's no longer my friend," said Jake flushed with anger and hurt.

After drying his hair, and giving him a consolatory hug, Grandma found two chairs, away from the battlefield, and a quieter place to talk. "Jake, Max is your best friend. You've had great times with him. I don't think he meant to hurt you. I think he was just playing and trying to be funny."

"Think about it Jake. You would be losing a good friend, losing the fun with a friend playing catch, running around the park, playing video games, eating pizza!"

For a few minutes you were wet, and now you're dry. It only lasted a few minutes, and so think about sacrificing your friendship—and not seeing Max again."

For a boy of seven, it was not what Jake expected to hear. Wasn't he supposed to stand up to an 'enemy' (real or imagined)? Shouldn't he or his father talk to Max or to Max's father? Shouldn't Max be punished? Grandma was telling him to remain friends, that the friendship was more important.

Jake thought about it for a while. He looked up at Grandma, and there was something about her face, a quiet smile, a reassuring hand to hold, and he thought about playing catch with Max, and the donut shop they both liked.

On the way home, Jake said only a few words, but the most meaningful were, "Okay, Grandma."

Perspective has a Latin root meaning to "look through" or "perceive," and "all the meanings of perspective have something to do with looking." (Cambridge English Dictionary)

And that meaning had everything to do with Jake, Lilla and Grandma looking at a building with a most bizarre structure. It had swirling curves, and a space created without any 90-degree angles. It sat in the middle of the city of rectangular and square buildings, and which was a museum.

Grandma explained that people came from all over the world to visit this extraordinary museum, filled with modern art, but also to appreciate this magnificent building that didn't have any stairs! "Don't you want to go inside?"

Both children agreed, categorically, they didn't want to go to a museum. But they thought they might like to see the inside when Grandma said they could start at the top of the building and go winding down the spirals to the ground. That sounded like fun.

Before they entered the museum, Grandma said she wanted to show them a picture that might help them see and understand the design of this great building. And so, the genie was solicited, and Grandma showed them a photograph, and several color pictures, of a mollusk called a nautilus shell. She then asked them to imagine the shell as they were going up in the elevator to the top—and there to look up!

It was another adventure quite unlike anything they had experienced before. When, hand-in-hand, Jake and Lilla reached the top of the Guggenheim Museum, they couldn't believe their eyes. They looked down at the spiraling floors, 1,450 feet long, and at the exotic triangular lighting, then looked up at the ceiling modeled on and inspired by a seashell! They were excited to start down the scrolling floors, slipping in between people staring at paintings, weaving in and out, down to the ground, only to start again, at the top.

But this time, Grandma insisted that they pause to look at and talk about the abstract paintings, the Mondrians, the Klees, the Kandinskys and (maybe) the current exhibition of Etel Adnan's' "Lights New Measure."

With some resistance, they stopped at the Kandinskys. Grandma happily, then, more persistently, pressed them to look at the colors and the shapes and what they thought. They stood in front of Kandinsky's 1913 painting, "Black Strokes." Grandma Fendell, trying to create interest, asked if any object in the painting looked like a snake.

If you've never seen a Wassily Kandinsky painting, imagine a collection (sometimes) of odd-shaped sticks, wandering balls, squiggles and loose threads floating and connecting in space. It would take a trained mind in any age group to understand them. The response from Jake was immediate and convincing. He squeezed his face into a most contorted expression of aversion. No art critic could have been more definitive!

The spiraling floors were the gym of their imagination, and Jake and Lilla wanted to romp in and out, down the spiraling rotunda, starting, of course, at the top. And so, down they quickly walked, threading their way to the elevator, with Grandma watching from above. There was joy in movement, ironically mimicked in the paintings, as the children descended again, hiding behind the columns to surprise Grandma when she completed her hurried walk down the floor.

Only in the small library of the Guggenheim did the adventurers stop briefly to draw pictures themselves, crayons provided, and then quickly protested that it was time to leave.

On the way home to the apartment on 75th street, Jake shared his critical assessment of the artwork to which he had been exposed in a singularly adamant statement, "I don't like Kandinsky!"

But both children agreed they did like fast-walking the floors and looking down from the top at all the people. They allowed that their time at the museum was not a total loss, and their appreciation was modestly increased by further discussion during a stop at the donut shop on the way home.

Chapter Eight

A Lesson in Manners at *Le Petite Maison* Restaurant

"Bon Jour, Madame et les enfants tres jolie. Une table pour trois pour le dejeuner?"

As the grandchildren, followed by Grandma, followed the hostess to the table, a waiter quickly appeared with three large menus.

Fortunately, some of the logistics and challenges of handling large menus with haute cuisine items had been studied beforehand. Studied by staring at the menu posted in the window of the restaurant, running fingers over the list till the children found something, at least, that sounded worthy of selection: "le Hamburger."

White tablecloth, quaint French charm, a waiter who treated the children respectfully, as he presented them and Grandmother with glasses of water, each with a lemon. After the proper protocol was followed, napkins placed on laps, and decorum all around, the fun began!

It was great good luck that Grandma chose to be seated away from other diners.

Even with the best effort at good manners, somehow Lilla knocked the full glass of water, ice, and lemon across the table in one stroke. While everyone hustled to dry the table and restore propriety, laughter, which the three diners tried to muffle with their hands cupped over their mouths, broke forth.

It was an opportunity for Grandma, who also was indecorously laughing, to introduce the topic of manners in general at restaurants.

Grandma Fendell, as the reader knows, had a talent for provoking attention by asking discerning questions and showing a knowledge of her audience.

"What would you NOT want to do if you were out on a date, Lilla and Jake, and wanted to show you had good manners at a restaurant? Let's see how many we can list?"

- *The first, of course, was, "Don't spill your water all over the table and/or on your date!"*
- *"If you want the waiter's attention, what do you not do?*

Not do: Scream, Hey Waiter!

Should do: Say, Excuse me, Would you…"

- *Not Do: Burp out loud.*

Should Do: Burp to yourself (with your hand or napkin over your mouth).

- *Not Do: Chew with your mouth open.*

Should do: Eat with your mouth closed.

- *Not Do: Get food all over your clothes.*

Should Do: Chewing with your mouth closed will prevent this indiscretion."

At this point in what had become a serious discussion, the topic became funnier and funnier.

"It was an opportunity for Grandma, who also was indecorously laughing, to introduce the topic of manners in general at restaurants."

- "Not Do: Emerge from the bathroom with your fly unbuttoned!

    Should Do: Check your zipper before exiting the bathroom.

- Not Do: Spit out soup that is too hot, too salty, or too distasteful.

    Should Do: Hold your napkin over your mouth and try to swallow the swill gracefully. Or, excuse yourself by nodding, and quickly go to the bathroom.

- Not Do: Accidently flatulate while laughing at your date's very funny joke!

    Should Do: Either pretend it never happened, or, excuse yourself profusely and hope for forgiveness.

- Not Do: Put so much food in your mouth that you begin to choke and unintentionally throw up in front of your date.

    Should Do: Cut your food into small bites, eating slowly and carefully.

By this time, les hamburgers consumed to the extent children finish their food, the laughter reached an embarrassing crescendo. To such an extent, the children and Grandmother placed their hands over their mouths (again) to muffle, if not entirely control, their hysterics.

As an astute reader must know, the solemnity of a church, a library, a courtroom or an upscale French restaurant, laughter that is impermissible can become more accelerated–hence more unacceptable-- in places where it is anathema!

By the time the chivalrous waiter had served most of the patrons in his area, Grandma and her fold had attained a more modest degree of composure in their entertainment and learning.

L'addition was presented, studied by Grandma, under the questioning eyes of the children, then paid, with appropriate acknowledgements of the waiter. With prepared farewell remarks by Grandma and the children, they departed. A bit happier? A bit wiser?

Such silliness, too, can bring remembered learning... as it did that day!

Conclusion

"'How many of you know what's important?... Henry Rackmeyer, you tell us what is important.'

'A shaft of sunlight at the end of a dark afternoon, a note of music, and the way the back of a baby's neck smells if its mother keeps it tidy,' answered Henry.

'Correct,' said Stuart. 'Those are the important things. You forgot one thing, though. Mary Bendix, what did Henry Rackmeyer forget?'

'He forgot ice cream with chocolate sauce on it', said Mary quickly.

'Exactly,' said Stuart."
— E.B. White, **Stuart Little**

"Stuart rose from the ditch, climbed into his car, and started up the road that led toward the north... As he peeked ahead into the great land that stretched before him, the way seemed long. But the sky was bright, and he somehow felt he was headed in the right direction."
— E.B. White, **Stuart Little** (Harper & Brothers, 1945)

Grandma Fendell is still at her post in a way of speaking. She is still providing alternative perspectives, into the worlds of science, of art and architecture, ancient history, literature and mathematics, sport and, of primacy, *play.*

In a zero-sum world, of right-and-wrong, good-and-bad, left-and-right, there is a grandmother who shows the wide varieties in the shades of grey. That the most well-regulated lives of children need dosages of improvisation, creativity, imagination, discovery of the unpredicted and unsubscribed age-appropriate seems axiomatic.

Because Lilla and Jake were born to discover the world, it is perhaps an act of wisdom to remember "ice cream with chocolate sauce on it" while they are "heading up the road that led toward the north…" More likely, I think, to true north.

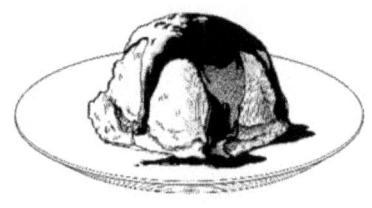

The End

About the Author

Charles Leahy spent a long career in corporate education where he presented workshops and consulted worldwide for MasterCard University, Asia Pacific Institute of Management Development, major international banks, telecoms, transportation, and many other clients.

He also enjoyed adventure travels, where he trekked mountain gorillas in the highlands of Uganda, found Komodo dragons in Indonesia, and encountered remote tribes in Papua New Guinea.

For his encore career, Leahy returned to his original calling, literature. He teaches courses on the British Novel, Travel Narratives and Colonialism, the Victorians, and recently *Banned Books: A Literary Study of Current Banned Novels* at local universities. Leahy holds a PhD in English from the University of California, Berkeley.